MW01297934

Śrī Gaurāṅga-Līlāmṛta

Śrī Gaurāṅga-Līlāmṛta

The Nectar Pastimes of the Golden Avatara

A Description of the Eight-fold Daily Pastimes of Lord Srī Chaitanya Mahāprabhu in the Eternal Realm of Śrī Navadvīpa-dhāma

Śrīla Viśvanātha Chakravartī Ṭhākura and his disciple Śrī Krishna Dāsa

Translation by Daśaratha-Suta Dāsa

Bookwrights Press
Charlottesville, VA

Published by Bookwrights Press.

Previously published by Nectar Books in 1992.

Printed in the United States of America

Painting in Dedication by Dhruva dasa

Other paintings and drawings by anonymous artists

ISBN: 978-1-880404-25-6

For Bulk orders email: info@bookwrightspress.com

Dedicated to our compassionate Spiritual Master,
His Divine Grace A.C. Bhaktivedanta Swami Prabhupāda,
who has fulfilled the mission of Lord Chaitanya by spreading the Holy Name to every town and village.

Contents

Introduction

All glories to Śrī Śrī Guru and Gaurāṅga!
All glories to the readers and relishers
of Śrī Gaurāṅga-Līlāmṛta!

We feel honored with the blessing of presenting *Śrī Gaurāṅga-Līlāmṛta* before the eyes of virtuous devotees of the Golden Avatār, Śrī Chaitanya Mahāprabhu. He is the united incarnation of the Divine Couple, Śrī Śrī Rādhā-Krishna, and has so kindly appeared in this world of darkness to illuminate it by His brilliant radiance of pure ecstatic love of Godhead.

Śrī Gaurāṅga-Līlāmṛta is an extremely rare book; very few libraries in India have copies of the manuscript, and even amongst Gauḍīya Vaishnavas, practically no one has ever seen it. The work is a result of the combined efforts of Śrīla Viśvanātha Chakravartī Ṭhākura and his disciple, Śrī Krishna Dāsa. Śrīla Chakravartīpāda had composed the first eleven verses in Sanskrit, known as *Śrīman-Mahāprabhor-Ashta-Kālīya-Līlā-Smaraṅa-Maṅgala-Stotram*; these are the seed-versas or *sūtras* that describe the eternal eight-fold daily pastimes of the fair-complexioned Lord. Then Śrī Krishna Dāsa composed Bengali verses that expound on these eleven verses to give a fuller, more detailed picture of the Lord's daily schedule. In writing the text, Krishna Dāsa often quotes verses or even entire songs from the *Chaitanya-Bhāgavat* of Śrīla Vrindāvana Dāsa Ṭhakura, plus songs written by Narahari Ghanashyāma (author of the *Bhakti-Ratnākāra*) and Lochana Dāsa Ṭhākura (author of *Chaitanya-Mangala*).

Śrī Krishna Dāsa, himself a great poet and scholar, also composed many other Bengali poetry-translations of Śrīla Viśvanātha Chakravartī's Sanskrit books, including *Mādhurya-Kādambinī*, *Chamatkāra-Chandrikā*, *Rāga-Vartma-Chandrikā*, *Bhāgavatāmrita-Kana*, *Bhakti-Rasāmrita-Sindhu-Bindhu*, and *Ujjvala-Nilamani-Kiraṇa*.

Thus Krishna Dāsa provided a priceless service to the Vaishnava community by allowing the Bengali devotees easy access to these jewel-like literatures, without their having to know the difficult intricacies of Sanskrit grammar.

This English poetry-translation is presented in a very simple way, for we have endeavored to preserve the innocence and charm of the original Bangali verses. Whenever the various names for the Lord occur, like Gorā, Vishvambhara, or Prabhu, they have been kept unchanged. We sincerely beg for the pleasure and blessings of the assembled devotees who appreciate our imperfect attempt. *JAI GAURA-NITĀI!*

–Daśaratha-Suta Dāsa
Śrī Gaura-pūrṇimā, 1992

Śrīman-Mahāprabhor-Aṣṭa-Kālīya-Līlā-Smaraṇa-Maṅgala-Stotram

Auspicious Prayers for Remembering the Eight-fold Daily Pastimes of Śrī Chaitanya Mahāprabhu

by Śrīla Viśvanātha Chakravartī Ṭhākura

THE GLORIES OF THE LORD'S DAILY PASTIMES

(1)

śrī-gaurāṅga-mahāprabhoś caraṇayor yā keśa-śeṣādibhiḥ
sevāgamyatayā sva-bhakta-vihitā sānyair yayā labhyate
tāṁ tan-mānasikīṁ smṛtiṁ prathayituṁ bhāvyāṁ sadā sattamair
naumi prātyahikaṁ tadīya-caritaṁ śrīman-navadvīpa-jaṁ

śrī-gaurāṅga-mahāprabhoś caraṇayoḥ – the feet of Śrī Gaurānga Mahāprabhu; *yā* – which; *ka-īśa-śeṣā-ādibhiḥ* – for Lord Brahmā, Lord Śiva and Lord Śesha; *sevā-agamyatayā* – by the imperceptible nature of devotional service; *sva-bhakta-vihitā* – accomplished by His own devotees; *sā-anyaih* – with others also; *yayā labhyate* – by which it is attainable; *tām* – them; *tat-mānasikīm smṛtim* – remembrance of Him within the mind; *prathayitum* – to be celebrated; *bhāvyām sadā* – to be contemplated always; *sattamaiḥ* – by the virtuous sages; **naumi** – I offer my obeisances; *prāthayahikam* – to the daily pastimes; *tadīya-caritam* – and His character; *śrīmat-navadvīpa-jam* – of the glorious Lord born in Navadvīpa.

Devotional service to the lotus feet of Śrī Gaurāṅga Mahāprabhu is far beyond the perception of Lord Brahmā, Lord Śiva, Lord Śesha-nāga and the rest, but it is continually indulged in by the Lord's own devotees, and is always available to other souls as well. Now I will begin my description of the process of *mānasī-sevā* (service to the Lord executed within the mind). This process is celebrated as continuous remembrance by the most virtuous sages. Therefore I offer my most respectful obeisances to the eternal daily life and pastimes of the Lord born in Navadvīpa.

BRIEF CODES DESCRIBING HIS DAILY SCHEDULE IN EIGHT PERIODS

(2)

rātryante śayanotthitaḥ sura-sarit-snāto babhau yaḥ prage
pūrvāhne sva-gaṇair lasaty upavane tair bhāti madhyāhnake
yaḥ pūryām aparāhnake nija-gṛha sāyaṁ gṛhe 'thāṅgane
śrīvāsasya niśā-mukhe niśi vasan gauraḥ sa no rakṣatu

rātri-ante – at the end of the night; *śayana-utthitaḥ* – having arisen from bed; *sura-sarit-snātah* – having bathed in the celestial river (Gaṅgā); *babhau* – shines; *yaḥ* – who; *prage* – in the morning; *pūrvāhne* – in the forenoon; *sva-ganaiḥ lasati* – enjoys with His own devotees; *upavane taiḥ bhāti* – remaining there splendidly in the gardens; *madhyāhnake* – at midday; *yaḥ* – who; *pūryām aparāhnake* – in the town during the afternoon; *nija-gṛhe* – to his own home; *sāyaṁ* – at dusk; *gṛhe* – at home; *atha aṅgane śrivāsasya* – thereafter in Śrīvāsa Paṇḍita's courtyard; *niśā-mukhe* – at the approach of evening; *niśi vasan* – stays at night; *gauraḥ saḥ* – that Gaura; *nahrakṣatu* – may he protect us.

(1) At the end of the night (before sunrise), Lord Śrī Chaitanya Mahāprabhu gets up from His bed, washes His face and converses with His wife. (2) In the morning, He is massaged with oil and bathes in the celestial Gaṅgā river, and then worships Lord Vishnu. (3) In the forenoon period, He enjoys discussing topics about Lord Krishna with His devotees during visits to their homes. (4) At midday, He enjoys pastimes in the gardens on the bank of the Gaṅgā. (5) In the afternoon, He wanders about the town of Navadvīpa, sporting with all the residents. (6) At dusk, He returns home to worship Lord Vishnu and be with His family. (7) In the evening, He goes with His associates to the courtyard of Śrīvāsa Paṇḍita to chant the holy names and dance in ecstasy. (8) At night, He returns home to take rest. May this Lord Gaura protect us all.

PERIOD 1 (3:36 – 6:00 A.M.)
PASTIMES AT THE END OF THE NIGHT

(3)

rātryante pika-kukkuṭādi-ninadaṁ śrutvā sva-talpotthitaḥ
śrī viṣṇu-priyayā samaṁ rasa-kathāṁ sambhāṣya santoṣya tāṁ
gatvā 'nyatra dharāsanopari vasan svadbhiḥ sudhautānano
yo mātrādibhir īkṣito 'ti-muditas taṁ gauram adhyemy ahaṁ

rātri-ante – at the end of the night; *pika-kukkuṭa-ādi-ninadaṁ* – the sound of cuckoos, roosters and others; *śrutvā* – hearing;

sva-talpa-utthitaḥ – getting up from his own bed; *śrī viṣṇu-priyayā samam* – with Śrī Vishnu-priya; *rasa-kathām* – talks about mellows; *sambhāṣya* – conversing; *santoṣya tāṁ* – pleasing her; *gatvā anyatra* – having gone elsewhere; *dharā-āsana-upari* – upon a seat; ***vasan*** – sitting; *svadbhiḥ* – with his own devotees; *su-dhauta-ānanaḥ* – nicely washed face; *yaḥ* – who; *mātrā-ādibhi-īkṣitah* – seen by his mother and others; *ati-muditaḥ* – extremely pleased; *tam gauram adhyemi ahaṁ* – I meditate on that Gaura.

At the end of the night, upon hearing the pleasant sounds made by many birds such as cuckoos, roosters, and others, Śrī Gaura arises from His bed. With His wife, Śrī Vishnu-Priyā, He discusses many topics concerning the transcendental mellows of Their mutual loving affairs, and thus They become very pleased. Then He gets up and goes to another room, wherein He sits upon a raised sitting place and is assisted by His devotees in washing His lotus face with nicely scented water. Thereafter, He very happily visits His mother, Śrī Śachī Devī, as well as other friends and relatives in the home. I meditate thus on the daily pastimes of Śrī Gaura.

PERIOD 2 (6:00 – 8:24 A.M.)
MORNING PASTIMES

(4)

prātaḥ svaḥ sariti sva-pārṣada-vṛtaḥ snātvā prasūnādibhis
tāṁ sampūjya gṛhīta-cāru-vasanaḥ srak-candanālaṅkṛtaḥ
kṛtvā viṣṇusamarcan-ādi sa-gaṇo bhuktvānnam ācamya ca
dvitraṁ cānya-gṛhe sukhaṁ svapiti yas taṁ gauram adhyemy ahaṁ

prātaḥ – in the morning; *svaḥ* – himself; *sariti* – in the river; *sva-pārṣada-vṛtaḥ* – surrounded by his associates; *snātvā* – bathed; *prasūnā-ādibhiḥ* – with flowers and other offerings; *tām* - he; *sampūjya* – fully worshiping; *gṛhīta-cāru-vasanaḥ* – putting on charming clothes; *srak-candana-alaṅkṛtaḥ* – decorated with flower garlands and sandalwood paste; *kṛtvā* – completing; *viṣṇu-samarcana-ādi* – worship of Lord Vishnu and so forth; *sa-gaṇaḥ* – with his devotees; *bhuktvā-annam acamya ca* – also having eaten and washed up; *dvitram* – next; *cā-anya-gṛhe* – and in another room; *sukham svapiti* – happily rests; yaḥ – who; *tam gauram adhyemi ahaṁ* – I meditate on that Gaura.

In the morning, after sunrise, the Lord goes with His associates to bathe in the holy river. While bathing, they also worship Mother Gaṅgā by offering flowers, incense and other presentations. They then come onto the bank of the river, where He is dressed with exquisite cloth and decorated with fresh flower garlands, sandalwood paste and other ornaments. Returning to His home in order to perform opulent worship of Lord Vishnu, as well as other rituals, they later partake of the foodstuffs that were offered to

Lord Vishnu. After washing His hands and mouth, Lord Gaura goes into another room and rests very happily for awhile. I meditate thus on the daily pastimes of Śrī Gaura.

PERIOD 3 (8:24 – 10:48 A.M.)
FORENOON PASTIMES

(5)

pūrvāhne śayanotthitaḥ su-payasā prakṣālya vaktrāmbujaṁ
bhaktaiḥ śrī-hari-nāma-kīrtana-paraiḥ sārddhaṁ svayaṁ kīrtayan
bhaktānāṁ bhavane 'pi ca sva-bhavane krīḍan nṛṇām vardhayaty
ānandaṁ pura-vāsināṁ ya urudhā taṁ gauram adhyemy ahaṁ

pūrvāhne – in the forenoon; *śayana-utthitaḥ* – arising from bed; *su-payasā prakṣālya* – washing with nice water; *vaktrā-ambujaṁ* – lotus face; *bhaktaiḥ* – with the devotees; *śrī-hari-nāma-kīrtana-paraiḥ* – with those fond of chanting the holy names of Lord Hari; *sārddham* – along with; *svayaṁ* – himself; *kirtayan* – performs congregational chanting; *bhaktānām bhavane* – at the devotees' homes; *api ca* – and also; *sva-bhavane* – at his own home; *krīḍat nṛṇām* – plays with the people; *vardhayaty ānandaṁ* – increases the bliss; *pura-vāsināṁ* – of the townsfolk; *yaḥ* – who; *urudhā* – greatly; *taṁ gauraṁ adhyemi ahaṁ* – I meditate on that Gaura.

Upon the arrival of the forenoon period, the Lord gets up from His nap and stretches His body. Then He washes His lotus face with sweetly scented water. Meeting with His devotees, who are all very fond of chanting Śrī Hari-nāma-kīrtana, He personally tastes and relishes the chanting of the holy names. Thus He sports, sometimes in the homes of various devotees, and sometimes in His own home. In this way, He increases the ecstatic pleasure of all the townspeople so much that it attains limitless heights. I meditate thus on the daily pastimes of Śrī Gaura-chandra.

PERIOD 4 (10:48 A.M. – 3:36 P.M.)
MIDDAY PASTIMES

(6)

madhyāhne saha taiḥ sva-pārṣada-gaṇaiḥ saṅkīrtayad-īdṛśaṁ
sādvaitendu-gadādharaḥ kila saha-śrīlāvadhūta-prabhuḥ
ārāme mṛdu-mārutaiḥ śiśiritair bhṛṅga-dvijair nādite
svaṁ vṛndā-vipinaṁ smaran bhramati yas taṁ gauram adhyemy ahaṁ

madhyāhne – at midday; *saha taiḥ* – with them; *sva-pārṣada-gaṇaiḥ*– with his own associates; *saṅkīrtyat-īdṛśaṁ* – chanting like this; *sa-advaita-indu* – with the moon-like Advaita; *gadādharaḥ* – and Gadādhara; *kila* – certainly; *saha-śrīla-avadhūta-prabhuḥ* – with the divine madman (Nityānanda Prabhu); *ārāme* – in the garden; *mṛdu-mārutaiḥ* – by gentle breezes; *śiśiritaih* – by cooling; *bhṛṅga-dvijaiḥ nādite* – by the sounds of bees and birds; *svaṁ vṛndā-vipinaṁ* – his own forest of Vrindāvan; *smaran* – remembering; *bhramati yaḥ* – who wanders; ***tam gauram adhyemi ahaṁ*** – I meditate on that Gaura.

During the midday period, Lord Chaitanya continues to enjoy the performance of intensely enthusiastic chanting and dancing, surrounded by His own dear devotees such as the moon-like Advaita Āchārya, Gadādhara Paṇḍita, and the divine madman,

Śrīla Nityānanda Avadhūta Prabhu. Afterwards, they all wander throughout the gardens and groves on the bank of the Gaṅgā, where they enjoy the sweet cooling breezes blowing over the river. Hearing the pleasant sounds of the bumblebees and birds in those gardens, the Lord remembers His own ecstatic pastimes as Rādhā and Krishna, which are occurring simultaneously in His own forest of Vrindāvan. I meditate thus on the daily pastimes of Śrī Gaura.

PERIOD 5 (3:36 – 6:00 P.M.) AFTERNOON PASTIMES

(7)

yaḥ śrīmān aparāhnake saha-ganais tais tādṛśaiḥ premavāṁs
tādṛkṣu svayam apy alāṁ tri-jagatāṁ śarmāṇi vistārayan
ārāmāt tata eti paura-janatā-cakṣuś cakoroḍupo
mātrā dvāri-mudekṣito nija-gṛhaṁ taṁ gauram adhyemy ahaṁ

yaḥ – who; *śrīmāt aparāhnake* – in the beautiful afternoon; *saha-gaṇaiḥ* – with his associates; *taiḥ tādṛśaiḥ* – like such; *premavām* – in a loving mood; *tādṛksu* – amongst those who are similar; *svayam api alām* – himself also so much; *tri-jagatām* – the three worlds; *śarmāṇi vistārayan* – expanding auspiciousness; *ārāmāt* – from the gardens; *tata* – thereafter; *eti* – He goes; *paura-janatā-cakṣuḥ cakora-uḍupaḥ* – the moon for the chakora-birds of the townspeople's eyes; *mātrā dvāri* – his mother at the door; *mudā-īkṣitaḥ* – happily seen; *nija-gṛham* – at his own home; *tam gauram adhyemi aham* – I meditate on that Gaura.

During the splendidly beautiful afternoon period, the Lord and His devotees all become equally maddened in ecstatic love, and thus they expand ever-increasing waves of auspicious benefit that ripple all throughout the three worlds. In this mood, they leave the gardens and travel back toward His home. Along the way, He satisfies the eyes of all the townspeople, just as the moon satisfies the *chakora* bird with its moonbeams. Reaching home, the Lord is met at the door by His mother and lavished with loving affection. I thus meditate on the daily pastimes of Śrī Gaura.

PERIOD 6 (6:00 – 8:24 P.M.)
SUNSET PASTIMES

(8)

yas tri-srotasi sāyam āpta-nivahaiḥ snātvā pradīpālibhiḥ
puṣpādyaiś ca samarcitaḥ kalita-sat-paṭṭāmbaraḥ srag-dharaḥ
viṣṇos tat-samayārcanaṁ ca kṛtavān dīpālibhis taiḥ samaṁ
bhuktvānnāni su-vīṭikām api tathā taṁ gauram adhyemy ahaṁ

yaḥ – who; *tri-srotasi* – in she who flows in three streams (the Gaṅgā); *sāyam āpta* – upon the arrival of dusk; *nivahaiḥ* – with the items; *snātvā* – having bathed; *pradīpālibhiḥ* – with lamps; *puṣpa-ādyaiḥ* – with flowers and so forth; *samarcitaḥ* – fully worshipped; *kalita-sat-paṭṭa-ambaraḥ* – putting on nice silken clothes; *srak-dharaḥ*– wearing garlands; *viṣṇoḥ tat-samaya-ārcanam* –

the worship of Lord Vishnu at that time; *ca* – also; *kṛtavān* – completing; *dīpālibhiḥ*– with lamps; *taiḥ samam* – with them; *bhuktvā annāni* – having eaten the grains; *su-vīṭikām* – and nice betel nuts; *api* – also; *tathā* – thereafter; *tam gauram adhyemi ahaṁ* – I meditate on that Gaura.

At dusk, the Lord bathes with His dear friends in the Gaṅgā, the river who flows in three streams. They devoutly worship the Gaṅgā by offering ghee lamps, flowers, and other articles. Afterwards, the Lord puts on fresh silken clothes and is adorned with flower garlands. Then, He worships Lord Vishnu at home by performing the evening *ārati* ceremony, offering ghee lamps and other items. Later, He and His friends partake of the foodstuffs and betel nuts that were offered to Lord Vishnu. I thus meditate on the daily pastimes of Śrī Gaura.

PERIOD 7 (8:24 – 10:48 P.M.) EVENING PASTIMES

(9)

yaḥ śrīvāsa-gṛhe pradoṣa-samaye hy advaita-candrādibhiḥ
sarvair bhakta-gaṇaiḥ samaṁ hari-kathā-pīyūṣam āsvādayan
premānanda-samākulaś ca cala-dhīḥ saṅkīrtane lampaṭaḥ
kartuṁ kīrtanam ūrdhvam udyama-paras tam gauraṁ adhyemy aham

yaḥ – who; *śrīvāsa-gṛhe* – in Śrīvāsa's home; *pradoṣa-samaye* – in the evening; *hi* – certainly; *advaita-candra-ādibhiḥ* – with Advaita-chandra and others; *sarvaiḥ bhakta-gaṇaiḥ samam* – with all the devotees; *hari-kathā-pīyūṣam āsvādayan* – tasting the nectar of Hari-kathā; *prema-ānanda-samākulaḥ* – very anxious in ecstatic loving bliss; *ca* – also; *cala-dhīḥ* – agitated mind; *saṅkīrtane lampaṭaḥ* – lustful for congregational chanting; *kartum* – to do; *kīrtanam ūrdhvam udyama-paraḥ* – fond of engaging in exalted, passionate chanting; *tam gauram adhyemi aham* – I meditate on that Gaura.

In the evening time, the Lord goes to the home of Śrīvāsa Paṇḍita, accompanied by Śrīla Advaita-chandra and other dear associates. Meeting with the multitude of His devotees, He tastes and relishes the nectar of topics about Lord Hari, and His mind becomes most agitated with the ecstasies of pure love of Godhead. Then, becoming very lustful to relish the congregational chanting of the holy names of the Lord, He orchestrates the performance of intensely jubilant *saṅkīrtana*, which attains the summit of passionate glorification of the Lord. I thus meditate on the daily pastimes of Śrī Gaura-sundara.

PERIOD 8 (10:48 P.M. – 3:36 A.M..) MIDNIGHT PASTIMES

(10)

śrīvāsāṅgana āvṛto nija-gaṇaiḥ sārddhaṁ prabhubhyāṁ naṭann
uccais tāla-mṛdaṅga-vādana-parair gāyadbhir ullāsayan
bhrāmyan śrīla-gadādhareṇa sahito naktaṁ vibhāty adbhutaṁ
svāgāre śayanālaye svapiti yas taṁ gauram adhyemy ahaṁ

śrīvāsa-aṅgana – in Śrīvāsa's courtyard; *āvṛtaḥ* – surrounded; *nija-gaṇaiḥ sārddhaṁ* – with his own devotees; *prabhubhyām naṭann* – by the two Lords dancing; *uccaiḥ tāla-mṛdaṅga-vādana-paraiḥ* – with those fond of playing loud *mridaṅga* drums; *gāyadbhih ullāsayan* – elated while singing; *bhrāmyan* – wandering; *śrīla-gadādhareṇa sahitaḥ* – with Śrīla Gadādhara; *naktam* – at night; *vibhāti* – shines; *adbhutam* – most astonishing; *sva-āgāre* – at his own home; *śayana-ālaye* – in his bedchamber; *svapiti* – sleeps; *yaḥ* – who; *tam gauram adhyemi ahaṁ* – I meditate on that Gaura.

Continuing well into the night, the Lord dances and dances with Prabhu Nityānanda in the courtyard of Śrīvāsa, surrounded by His most intimate devotees. His ecstatic singing is accompanied by the devotees who are expert in playing very loud rhythms on the *mridaṅga* drums. He wanders and dances with Śrī Gadādhara Prabhu in the most astonishing way throughout the night, until just before dawn. Then He returns to His own home, where He retires to His bed chamber and falls asleep. I thus meditate on the daily pastimes of Śrī Gaura.

The Benefit of Reciting This Prayer

(11)

śrī-gaurāṅga-vidhoḥ sva-dhāmani navadvīpe 'ṣṭa-kālodbhavāṁ
bhāvyāṁ bhavya-janena gokula-vidhor līlā-smṛter āditaḥ
līlāṁ dyotayad etad atra daśakaṁ prītyānvito yaḥ paṭhet
taṁ prīṇāti sadaiva yaḥ karuṇayā taṁ gauram adhyemy ahaṁ

śrī-gaurāṅga-vidhoḥ – of the moonlike Śrī Gaurāṅga; *sva-dhāmani navadvīpe* – in his own abode of Navadvīpa; *aṣṭa-kāla-udbhavām*– manifesting in eight time periods; *bhāvyām* – fit for meditating upon; *bhavya-janena* – by those inclined towards meditating; *gokula-vidhoḥ līlā-smṛteḥ āditaḥ* – before remembering the pastimes of the moon over Gokula (Lord Krishna); *līlām* – the pastimes; *dyotayat etat* – these radiantly shining; *atra daśakaṁ* – these ten verses; *prītyā-anvitaḥ* – filled with love; *yaḥ paṭhet* – whoever reads; *tam prīṇāti* – pleases Him; *sadā eva* – perpetually; *yaḥ karuṇayā* – by whose mercy; *tam gauram adhyemi aham* – I meditate on that Gaura.

Śrī Gaurāṅga, the Moon over Navadvīpa, is manifest in His own abode during eight periods of each and every day. His pastimes during these periods should first be remembered by meditative devotees before they visualize the simultaneously-occurring pastimes of Śrī Krishna, the Moon over Gokula. If someone lovingly reads or recites the Lord's eternal daily pastimes as they are illuminated in the ten verses of this prayer, then the Lord is perpetually pleased with that person, by His own merciful compassion. I thus meditate on the daily pastimes of Śrī Gaura.

Śrī Gaurāṅga-Līlāmṛta

Jaya gaura nityānanda jayādvaita-chandra
gadādhara śrīvasādi gaura-bhakta-vrinda

vande 'ham śrī-śachī-sūnuṁ gaura-chandraṁ mahāprabhuṁ
nityānanda-prabhuṁ śrīmad advaitaṁ tad-gaṇaiḥ saha

"I offer my respectful obeisances unto the divine son of mother Śachī, the fair-complexioned moon-like Gaura Mahāprabhu, along with His own associates Nityānanda Prabhu and Śrīmad Advaita."

First I offer my obeisances unto the feet of my *guru* and
the *Vaishnavas*, for their mercy sustains me
in life or in death.
Glory, glory to Gaura-Chandra, the darling boy of Śachī!
Glory, glory to my very own Nityānanda Prabhu!
Glory to Śrī Advaita and Gadādhara,
the oceans of compassion!
Glory to Śrīvāsa and all the other devotees,
the friends of the fallen!

Holding the lotus feet of Śrī Guru within my heart
I shall briefly narrate *Gaurāṅga-Līlāmṛta.*
This description of the Lord's pastimes
as they flow throught eight periods of the day
(ashta-kāla) is very relishable.

Please listen now as I present the song outlining the Lord's pastimes in eight periods:

(to be sung in rāga Tudī)

(1) First Period: *Nishānta-Līlā* Pastimes at the End of Night

(3:36 – 6:00 A.M., sunrise)

niśi-śeṣe gorā, ghumera āveśe,
śayana pālaṅkopare
heno-jana nāhi, je bārek se śobhā,
heriyā parāṇa dhare

At the end of the night Gorā lies upon a nice bed under the spell of sleep. There is no person alive who could behold such splendor and retain his life-breath.

(2) Second Period: *Prātah-Līlā* Morning Pastimes

(6:00 – 8:24 A.M.)

prabhāte jāgiyā, nija-parikara,
veṣtita aṅgane vasi
jaga-jana mana, helāya hariyā
hiyāte thākaye paśi

Waking up in the morning, He sits in the courtyard surrounded by His intimate associates. Effortlessly enchanting the minds of all beings in the universe, He penetrates into their hearts and remains there always.

danta-dhāvanādi, sāri sura-nadī,
snānādi ānandāveśe
nija-gṛha gana- saha je bhojana,
kautuka śayana śeṣe

After brushing His teeth and so forth, He bathes in the celestial river Gaṅgā, overcome with ecstatic bliss. Then back at His own home, He takes breakfast with His associates, sporting novel prankish fun, and afterwards rests.

(3) Third Period: *Purvāhna-Līlā* Fore-noon Pastimes

(8:24 – 10:48 A.M.)

purvāhna samaye, śuklāmbara ādi,
bhakata-gaṇera ghare
premera āveśe, avaśa hoiyā,
vividha vilāsa kore

In the fore-noon period. He visits the homes of devotees like Shuklāmbara and others, and becomes totally overwhelmed, immersed in ecstatic love as He sports various pastimes.

(4) Fourth Period: *Madhyāḥna-Līlā* Midday Pastimes

(10:48 A.M. – 3:36 P.M.)

madhyāhna-kālete, ati manohara,
puṣpera kānana-mājhe
kota kota raṅge, taraṅge vibhora,
saṅge pariṣada sāje

In the midday period He goes to an extremely enchanting flower garden and becomes absorbed in riding the sportive waves of limitless pastime after pastime along with His intimate associates.

(5) Fifth Period: *Aparāhna-Līlā* Afternoon Pastimes

(3:36 – 6:00 P.M.)

aparāhna-kāle, priya-gaṇa mili,
bhuvana-mohana veśa
nadīyā-nagare, phire ghare ghare,
śobhāra nāhiko śeṣa

In the afternoon He meets with His beloved friends and dresses in garments that enchant all the worlds. Wandering throughout the town of Nadīyā to each and every house, He displays wondrous glory that has no end.

(6) Sixth Period: *Sāyam-Līlā* Dusk Pastimes

(6:00 – 8:24 P.M.)

sandhya-kāle nija- bhavane gamana,
ati aparūpa rīta
deva vandanādi, koraye jatane,
jāhāte māyera prīta

At dusk He returns to His own home in the most astonishing manner and endeavors carefully to worship the deity, which pleases His mother very much.

(7) Seventh Period: *Pradosha-Līlā* Evening Pastimes

(8:24 – 10:48 P.M.)

pradoṣe śrīvāsa- mandire praveśa,
adhika ullāsa hiyā
tathā priya-gaṇa, mana anurūpa,
koraye adbhuta kriyā

In the evening He goes to Śrīvāsa's house while His heart blossoms in great delight. There He performs amazing pastimes according to the wishes of His dear friends.

(8) Eighth Period: *Nisha-Līlā* Night Pastimes

(10:48 P.M. – 3:36 A.M.)

niśaye sakala, parikara saha,
sukhe saṅkīrtana kori
punaḥ āsi nija- priyāra mandire,
bhane dāsa...

At night He happily performs *saṅkīrtana* along with His closest associates. Later He goes to the home of His beloved wife. Thus narrates Krishna Dāsa.

ONE

Nishānta-Līlā Pastimes at the End of the Night

(3:36 - 6:00 A.M.)

The Beauty and Splendor of Śrī Gaurāṅga in His Sleeping Chamber

At the end of the night Gorā-Chanda is in His
sleeping chamber.
His limbs twitch as Cupid churns His mind.
The golden bedstead is inlaid with solid coral
and is decorated with pillows covered
with pure white cloth.
The nicely-colored silk is secured by cords in four
corners, and the jewelled tassels emit pinkish rays
in all directions.
Tall, strong golden posts grace the four corners
supporting the expansive canopy hanging overhead.
Swinging from all edges are long strands of very tiny
pearls which appear like the celestial river flowing
down from the heavens.

The bedstead appears just like the nicely-formed peak of Mt. Kailāsa, while the splendorous bolsters, appear like balls of fresh cream.

Covering the mattress is pure white silk, in the middle of which slumbers Gorā Dvija-maṇi, the jewel of the twice-born *brāhmaṇas.*

His long limbs put to shame the luster of molten gold, while overwhelmed with the moods of lazy lounging He rolled over until He was lying on His stomach.

His hair hangs in bunches of curly locks as His slackened pearl necklace lies tangled with His jasmine garland.

The upward lines of His beautiful *tilak* shine with the splendor of sandalwood paste.

Around His face the dots of *kunkum* and musk are enchanting.

Jewelled earrings rest against His glistening cheeks, while the arch of His eyebrows conquers the arrows of Cupid.

Attempting to find a suitable comparison for the splendor of Gaurāṅga's closed eyes, even the Creator with all his skills of supremely refined craftsmanship is baffled to the utmost extent of his imagination.

I can understand that Kāmadeva has vanished in fear of the crooked arch of Gorā's eyebrows; becoming bodiless, Cupid is therefore called Anaṅga.

Who has created this form of Lord Gaurāṅga's?

It is like Cupid's net for ensnaring the innocent deer that are the hearts of chaste girls.

His two lotus-like eyes are closed in repose. His thick black eyelashes are motionless.

His splendidly-colored lips defeat the hue of *bimba*-fruits while His slightly smiling mouth enraptures the universe.

His broad chest is beautified by numerous necklaces, and His arms, extending to His knees, are very muscular.

His arms are adorned with bracelets of nine jewels, and His divine form is beautified with thick patches of sandalwood paste.

His hips are wrapped with very fine white cloth, while His upper body is partially covered with a splendorous cloth, the border of which is woven in ornate golden flowers.

His thin *brāhmana* thread is visible there, supremely pure and white.

The palms of His hands are reddish like blooming water-lotuses, and the sparkling auras of His finger-rings destroy darkness all around.

The nicely-constructed golden temple is pervaded with happiness.

On the four sides are four bejeweled terraces with gazebos.

On top of the temple are flags and golden jugs and strands of pearls so large that they look like full moons.

Both sides of the temple are beautified by eight crystal pillars supporting rows of swans formed of silver.

In four directions are four gates studded with jewels and
inlaid here and there with emeralds.

The golden doors shine with their solid coral bolts, and
crystal cornices glitter like rows of candles.

Ranks of huge mirrors are fixed on the walls, and they
are painted with scenes of the mellow-sports
of Rādhā and Krishna.

These spotless mirrors are also embellished here and
there with artificial flower-trees and lotus flowers
with hundreds of petals.

These ornamentations on the mirrors radiate a luster so
much like real lotuses that swarms of bumblebees
wander here mistaking them for actual lotus-groves.

The four directions shine with eight round windows
on the doors, which are expert in mocking
the orb of the sun.

These round windows are lined with brilliant sunstones
that are bordered on the inside and outside edges
with rubies.

The temple's altar, vestibule, courtyard, and staircases
are beautifully formed of solid crystal slabs.

Within the temple, by the sleeping-chamber,
is a flower-garden.

Sitting upon branches here and there are cuckoos
and other birds.

The cool breeze flows with the pleasant fragrances of
various flowers while the branches of the trees
sway along ever so gently.

Hanging upon the door of this inner chamber is the
lovely sight of shoes, umbrella and pure white
chāmara whisk.
On both sides of the bed are golden tables supporting
jewelled boxes containing betel-nut packets
and golden pitchers full of scented water.
On the floor in front of these tables is a beautiful place
for rinsing the mouth.

Gaurāṅga is Awakened

Overcome with the fatigue of sporting vigorous *kīrtana*,
the moonlike Gaura-Shashi sleeps upon the bed.
In the corner of the room sits a parrot in a golden cage.
Seeing that the night has ended,
the parrot becomes restless.
With a blissful mind he thinks to himself,
"*I will wake Gaurāṅga*," as his wings blossom with
thrill-bumps and his eyes flow with tears.
He calls out with a very sweet voice,
"Arise, Gaura-Rāya!
The dew is settling upon the morning.
Seeing the approaching pink of the rising sun,
the bumblebees have abandoned their resting-place
in the lotus flowers.
Seeing the directions illumined with glorious light,
the she-herons have arisen and playfully come
to mingle with the he-herons.

The swans and cranes and other water-dwelling birds
have all gone to the bank of the celestial
Sura-dhūni river.
All the birds headed by the doves have begun their
cooing and chirping, and the people stir about the
town, seeing to their own work.
The he-deer and she-deer have left their formation
and wander in smaller groups for grazing on
fresh grasses."

His sleep broken upon hearing the words of the parrot,
His two lotus eyes open ever so slightly.
In His mind He is fully aware of the *kuñja-līlā*
of Vrindāvana, and thus meditating on the dawn
pastimes performed by Rādhā and Krishna
in Their bowerhouse, He remains motionless
and pretends to continue sleeping.

In another room sleeps Śrīmatī Vishnu-Priyā Devī,
who quickly gets out of her bed upon seeing
the arrival of morning.
She walks slowly in drowsiness and goes to Śachī's
courtyard while her eyes roll to and fro.
Hearing the sweet relishable sound of Vishnu-Priyā's
anklets and ornaments, Śachī opens the door
and steps outside to greet her.
Seeing her daughter-in-law, she speaks in pleasant
words, "I am busy with household chores now.
You may go and bathe in the Sura-dhūni."

Then, in order to pamper her son, Śachī proceeds very quickly with anxious mind.

Entering His sleeping-chamber, she silently comes before His bed.

Stroking His divine form very, very tenderly with her hand, she considerately speaks in a soft and gentle voice,

> "Arise, dear son Gorā-Chanda, it is morning. The townspeople have arisen and are sitting outside in anticipation. Śrīvāsa and all the other devotees are very anxiously waiting to see you. Please get up and quickly start on the path. Give up your sleep, arise and go wash your face."

The Lord Begins His Day

Hearing His mother's words, Gorā-Raya stretches His body and sits up in the bed.

At this moment, Sītā Ṭhākurāṇī (the wife of Śrī Advaita) arrives along with Mālinī (the wife of Śrīvāsa Paṇḍita) and other chaste wives of the devotees.

Having all come and met together at Śachī's home, they enter Gaurāṅga's sleeping chamber.

All the ladies of the town also proceed there with anxious minds just to have *darshan* of Gaurāṅga.

Mother Śachī lights a ghee-lamp scented with camphor on a golden tray, then jubilantly places it in the hands of Mālinī, who offers it as *ārati* to the gorgeous Gaurāṅga-Sundara.

The male servants attentively bring in a golden footstool, full water pitchers, a tongue scraper, tooth powder, and so forth. Leaving the room, Gorā comes out into the courtyard.

Going to another room in the house, He conducts His morning activities.

Then He comes out and sits down with His feet upon a footstool.

After brushing His teeth and other duties, He goes and sits on a very elevated sitting place.

Then His devotees, who have also just finished their morning practices, begin to arrive–Prabhu Nityānanda, Śrī Advaita, Gadādhara, Mukunda, Murāri, Haridāsa, Vakreshvara, Shuklāmbara Brahmachārī, Śrīdhara and others.

Coming together at the Lord's house, all the devotees successively offer their respects at His feet in the appropriate manner.

Then Prabhu Nityānanda comes and sits to the Lord's right with Gadādhara on the left, and the devotees on all four sides.

Before Them sits Advaita, the Lord of Shānti-pura.

What splendor manifests here! It cannot even be described with words!

Description of Śrīmatī Vishnu-Priyā's Beauty

Then Vishnu-Priyā Devī very playfully goes in the company of her girlfriends to bathe in the Sura-dhūni river.

The complexion of her body conquers that of a golden lotus and her most lovely face radiates the splendor of how many moons?

Her braid graces her hips like a great snake, and it is bound with golden threads interwoven with strands of bakula flowers.

Her wavy locks appear to be swarms of bumblebees, and her two cheeks sparkle like mirrors.

Her ears are adorned with jewel-studded earrings, swinging from which are tiny ornaments inlaid with pearls. To support the weight of this extraordinary ear-ornament, a golden chain is fastened to a post in her earlobe and loops over her ear.

The part in her hair is bordered by tiny pearls tied on golden threads and interspersed with rubies. On her forehead is a dot of *sindura* tinted reddish like the rising sun, both sides of which are embellished with designs drawn in dark musk. Further designs in musk beautify her cheeks, and her pleasingly-colored lips form an enchantingly gentle smile. Her fickle eyes dart about like the movements of a wagtail bird, as Cupid himself trembles in fear to see the movements of her eyebrows.

Her nose conquers the beauty of the sesame flower,
and an elephant-pearl dangles from it.

Around her neck is an ornamental necklace
interwoven with jasmine garlands.
From her neck descends a splendorous array
of golden necklaces arranged in successive loops
from small to large.
The beauty of her breasts puts to shame
that of golden water pitchers, and they are encircled
with *champaka* flowerbuds.
Her breasts are adorned with vines drawn in
sandalwood paste and bordered with strands
of precious elephant-pearls.
Her two arms appear as golden lotus-stems
and they are decorated with conchshell-bangles
and other ornaments.
Her upper arms are encircled by armlets that are
bordered with silk, dangling from which
are golden charms.
From her reddish palms extend fingers adorned with
rings, and her index finger shines with a golden
ornament that is studded with tiny mirrors.
Her entire form is made lustrous by her divine
raincloud-colored silken cloth, its border studded
with sparkling jewels and precious *jārī* weavings.
Her hips are broad and her waist is slim.
Orchid-jewels playfully dance upon her ornamental belt.

Her feet are decorated with reddish lac-dye,
and her anklebells are trimmed with jewels.
Her sweet gait mocks that of a royal swan as her anklets
resound like the chirping of sparrows.
Her entire body ridicules the softness of fresh cream.

Amidst jokes and laughter she bathes in the Sura-dhuni.

Thus Ends the Nishānta-Līlā

TWO

Prātah-Līlā
Morning Pastimes

(6:00 – 8:24 A.M.)

The Cooking Begins

Returning home, Vishnu-Priyā changes her clothes and begins arranging the paraphernalia for *Vishnu-pūjā*. Śachī Ṭhākurāṇī quickly completes her own bath, and seeing that it is late, goes home as fast as possible.

Then Sītā Devī, Mālinī and the wives of all the dear devotees also finish their baths and proceed at once to Śachī's home.

Going inside, they carefully receive the finest items to offer the Lord that are brought from their homes by maidservants.

Śachī Mātā takes the items along and, washing her feet, enters the kitchen. Approaching Vishnu-Priyā Devī, Śachī says, "It is so late! Alas! Please begin cooking!"

Very happy in her mind to receive this order, Vishnu-Priyā immediately goes and sits down to cook.

All the cooking duties performed by Mālinī are directed by the gestures of Sītā Ṭhākurāṇī.

First they cook sweet rice. Upon its completion, it is transferred to a new container.

Numerous types of spinach are prepared then arum-root, eggplant and many other items.

Assorted vegetables are minced and spiced with black pepper. Pigeon-pea soup is made with dried mango pieces.

Many varieties of curries soaked in ghee are kept separately.

Ground kidney-bean patties and ground pigeon-pea patties are nicely fried in ghee.

Coconut-cereal is fried along with cakes made from flowers.

There are different kinds of eggplant mixed with sesame seeds.

Much effort and attention is given to all this cooking. The sweet and the sour preparations are kept separately.

Ground kidney-bean patties are soaked in sour yogurt then mixed with cumin and black pepper and are fried.

They make varieties of sweet pies with farina. Sprinkling them with ghee, they are carefully stored.

Milk-film is stuffed with creamy curd, sugar and spices, and is fried.

They make so many items that it is impossible to describe them all!

A great quantity of the finest rice is nicely cleaned
and cooked in limitless different styles.
In another house someone churns milk, while elsewhere
others prepare sweetmeats and cooked vegetables.
Farina is kneaded with sugar and carefully rolled
into laddhus.
Wheat is formed into coils, fried in ghee and soaked
in sweet juice.
Cheese and condensed milk is kneaded with sugar
and formed into laddus shaped like pomegranates.
They make sweets from pumpkin, and also
disc-shaped crispy cakes.
Large quantities of cucumber and chick-peas
are fried in ghee.
Milk is cooked down until it forms very thick *kshīra,*
then it is poured into new clay pots; cardamom,
camphor, black pepper and so forth are added
and it is immediately put away to cool.

Some squash are cooked in milk, others in yogurt.
Ghee without salt is used to fry celestial spinach.
Delicious ginger-curd sweets are prepared
from sesame powder.
They are sprinkled with ghee and placed to soak
in clay pans of yogurt.
Magnolia and banana sweets are made with
thickly condensed milk.

Numerous varieties of out-of-season fruits are somehow produced. Sherbets are made from pomegranate, lotus flowers and sugarcane.

On top of these are placed coconut pieces carved in different shapes.

Oranges, almonds, mashed date-balls, lemons, grapes and custard-apples are mixed with profuse quantities of cream.

Cereals are meticulously prepared from pigeon-peas and chick-peas.

The night before they had been ground and soaked in water.

Salt is crushed and kept separately. Numerous kinds of pickles are brought to the house from elsewhere.

Ripe mango pieces are marinated in sugar-sauce. Śachī has been keeping them soaking for many days.

There are mustard-powder soup, plum pickles, and many more things that are brought and placed outside.

Then Śachī Devī comes into the kitchen and is overjoyed to view the assortment of cooked preparations.

She addresses her daughter-in-law, "What is the delay with the cooking?"

Vishnu-Priyā is embarrassed and does not say a word in reply.

So Mālinī speaks up, "Oh Śachī Devī! The cooking is finished. There is no more delay."

Śachī says, "Good! I have personally cleaned Lord Vishnu's eating-room with my own hands.

Now I am quickly going to arrange the offering there."
Saying this, she goes outside and says to Īshana, "Please ask Vishvambhara to immediately take His bath in the Gaṅgā.
It is upsetting my mind that we are so late today – the rice and cooked vegetables are getting cold!"

Mahāprabhu Goes to Bathe in the Gaṅgā

Īshana goes and addresses the Lord, "Mātā has asked me to tell you to go bathe in the Gaṅgā now."
Hearing this, Mahāprabhu feels very blissful in His mind and leaves with His devotees for bathing.
The devotees gather flower garlands, ground sandalwood pulp, scented oil for massaging His body, and clean clothes as they depart for the river.
Along the way, He has many conversations with the devotees.
Then, in their company Śrī Gaurāṅga Rāya enters the waters of the Gaṅgā and offers His obeisances unto her.

[From the *Chaitanya-Bhāgavat*]

"Who could possibly describe the opulence of Nadīyā?
At one bathing place, thousands and thousands of people bathe.
Some are peaceful saints, some austere ascetics, some sannyāsīs.

I don't know how many children come there
and mix in the crowds!
The Jāhnavī (Gaṅgā) encircles the Lord on all sides,
and He secretly offers her own water unto her ripples.
On the plea of making waves, the Jāhnavī dances,
even though her feet are served by residents
of limitless universes.
Navadvīpa Rāya played water-sports in the Gaṅgā river
while the residents of Nadīyā looked on in the
greatest fortune.
As Prabhu Vishvambhara played in the waters of the Gaṅgā,
He looked just like the full moon itself
playing in the ocean.
All the fortunate souls who had come to the landing to bathe
incessantly beheld the face of Vishvambhara."

One male servant comes forward to massage the Lord,
attentively rubbing and cleansing His body.
Then Prabhu bathes in the company of His devotees,
and they ascend the riverbank with much
playful sporting.
Another *dāsa* comes forward to wipe His body dry,
carefully disentangling and dressing His hair.
Helping Him change into dry clothes, he adorns Him
with divine flower garlands, sandalwood paste,
and ornaments for each and every limb.

The Offering

On returning home, Prabhu Gaurāṅga Śrī Hari washes His feet and enters the temple room of Lord Vishnu.

[From the *Chaitanya-Bhagavat*]

"Gaura Bhagavān properly performs Vishnu-pūjā.
Offering water with Tulasī, He then offers obeisances."

Then Prabhu comes and sits upon a golden platform and offers the sweetmeats to Lord Vishnu.

Śachī Devī carefully brings the items on golden plates and places them before her son.

Offering scented water from a golden vessel, He sits alone and feeds the Lord some nice edibles.

All the devotees headed by Nityānanda Prabhu, Advaita Gosai, Narahari, Gadādhara, Śrīvāsa, Rāmāi, Vakreshvara, Haridāsa and others had returned to their own homes after bathing in the Gaṅgā.

Each performing their own morning duties, they again come together to meet at Prabhu's house.

Then Vishnu-Priyā Devī finishes her cooking.

On Śachī's order she goes to the offering-room and places various types of rice on many golden plates; lining them up in mound after mound, she sprinkles them with ghee.

All the vegetable preparations that were cooked are piled alongside the rice in successive order.

All the cooked grains as well as all the pickled items are arranged in row after row according to the progression of their taste.

Water is poured into a golden vessel and is scented with camphor.

The finest betel nuts are made pleasant by adding cloves and cardamom and are put into a bejeweled box.

Placing Tulasī-*mañjarīs* upon the grains, she offers the food to the Shāligrām while giving Him *āchamana*.

The Morning Meal

Then Śachī Devī very jubilantly calls her son and His friends to eat.

Nityānanda accompanies the Lord and His devotees as they quickly come.

Gaura-Chandra washes His feet and sits upon a majestic seat.

Nityānanda and Gadādhara sit on either side of Him while Advaita and Śrīvāsa sit facing them.

All the devotees sit in the courtyard while Śachī blissfully serves them.

Again and again she brings and serves all the cooked offerings.

Overwhelmed with affection, she makes them eat while
all their chaste wives stand and watch from afar.
Prabhu laughs and jokes while He eats,
as the male servants bring and serve water.

Washing His mouth, He goes and sits on an *āsana*
as all the devotees sit surrounding Him on all sides.
Prabhu eats betel nuts and laughs while some attendants
serve Him by waving *chāmara* whisks.

Then Sītā Devī gathers Mālinī and the devotees' wives,
Śachī comes forward and seats them all,
feeding them to the great delight of her heart.
After eating, the wives return to their own homes,
and Śachī finally eats along with Vishnu-Priyā.
They wash their mouths and go to sit in a solitary place
as the servants headed by Īshana come
for their own meal.

The servants then clean the house. After washing all the
pots and plates, they put them away.
Nityānanda and the other devotees go to take
a little rest.
Seeing His devotees off, Prabhu Vishvambhara enters
the sleeping chamber.
Lying on His bed, He drifts to sleep while some dear one
massages His feet.

A few devotees headed by Gadādhara and Narahari also rest along with the Lord in His house.

The servant of the servant of Śrī Gaurāṅga and Nityānanda, Krishna Dāsa, narrates the Lord's pastimes.

Thus Ends the Prātaḥ-Līlā

THREE

Purvāhna-Līlā Forenoon Pastimes

(8:24 – 10:48 A.M.)

Waking Up From the Nap

After a short while Prabhu Vishvambhara awakens
and sits up in bed.

The other devotees headed by Gadādhara also wake up
and are served water brought in golden pitchers
by the male servants.

Then Prabhu washes His face and sits down
with a supremely blissful mind.

After resting briefly, all the devotees carefully attend
their own duties.

They are very eager to meet with the Lord, but knowing
it is not time yet, they do not go to Him.

Some of them deliberate on the *Bhāgavat-shāstra*.
Some of them mingle in Advaita's room.

Some of them gather in groups of five or seven
and perform *kīrtan* while clapping their hands.

Thus the devotees associate together, each in
their own way.

Later all the *bhaktas* headed by Śrīvāsa arrive at Prabhu's house.

Offering obeisances at the Lord's feet, they stay on the ground, but the Lord embraces them all and makes them sit nicely.

Visiting The Devotees' Homes

Then in the company of Gadādhara and the others Prabhu proceeds to Shuklāmbara's house in a mood of great sportive fun.

[From the *Chaitanya-Bhāgavat*]

"He incessantly remained in the company of Gadādhara; indeed, Prabhu could not be separated from Gadādhara for even a moment."

Shuklāmbara Brahmachārī sees his own Lord and respectfully gets up, abandoning whatever he is doing.

Bowing at His feet, he washes them and seats Prabhu on an elevated *āsana*.

Nityānanda and Gadādhara sit by His side while Advaita and all the other devotees sit facing them.

Shuklāmbara's house is close by the Jāhnavī river.

There sports Gorā of beautiful body. The bank of the Sura-dhūni is lined with rows of *kadamba* trees.

There are thousands and thousands of peacocks,
cuckoos and bees buzzing.

The Lord's mind is overwhelmed with the remembrance
of the Yamuna river, and He has a vision of Krishna
herding cows in the pastures.

Thus He calls out with great feeling, *"O Śrīdāma! Sudāma!
Stoka-Krishna! He Arjuna! O Brother Balarāma!"*

Seeing Prabhu's condition, the hearts of Gadādhara
and the others are overcome with ecstasy
as their eyes brim with tears.

In this mood they sport numerous pastimes.

Then Gaurāṅga Śrī Hari gets up and quickly proceeds
to Śrīdhara's house. Seeing Gaura arrive
along with His associates, Śrīdhara gets up.

Offering water at their feet, he bows down respectfully.
Mahāprabhu sits with blossoming face
as His devotees surround Him on all sides.

He laughs and converses with Śrīdhara.

Seeing He of such enchanting beauty with Śrīdhara,
I can find no words and become a little stunned.

Staying at Śrīdhara's house for a short while,
Prabhu gets up and leaves, walking in the manner
of a maddened baby elephant.

[From the *Chaitanya-Bhāgavat*]

*"Prabhu perpetually goes to everyone's house and reveals
to them the visions of Chatur-bhuja (four-armed form),
Ṣaḍ-bhuja (six-armed form) and so forth.*

At one moment He goes to Gaṅgādāsa Murāri's home, and at the next moment He goes to Āchārya-Ratna's home."

Then Prabhu takes His devotees and sits in a heavenly flower garden.

The servant of the servant of Śrī Gaurāṅga and Nityānanda, Krishna Dāsa, narrates the Lord's pastimes.

Thus Ends the Purvāhna-Līlā

FOUR

Madhyāhna-Līlā
Midday Pastimes

(10:48 A.M. – 3:36 P.M.)

Description of the Flower Garden

In this way Gaura-Chandra comes to the flower garden
and beholds the splendor of the forest
with His red-tinged eyes.

This flower garden is a grandly expansive place. In all
four directions are groups of very tall *kadamba* trees.

At the base of these *kadamba* trees are dense screwpine
bushes which are encircled by thorns.

Seeing this thorny forest from afar, the common people
never come here.

Mādhavī and *mālatī* jasmine-vines climb up
and embrace the *kadamba* trees.

The pleasant south wind blows, carrying flower-pollen
with its breezes.

In four directions are four paths formed with jewels. In
two directions are beautiful rows of *bakula* trees.

The forest blooms with small white *kunda*-jasmine buds,
oleander, red amaranth, *tagara* flower-trees,

groups of jewelled gardenias, *nāgeshvara* flowers,
and many other varieties of fragrant jasmines
like *jātī*, *yūthī*, and *mallikā*.

Bakula trees, clove-pink vines, pink trumpet-flowers,
and guelder-roses are beautifully manifest
in row after row.

White lilies, yellow magnolias, and many red flame-trees
are blooming.

Here and there are seen very enchanting jewelled altars,
above which the trees and creepers are formed
like canopies.

The dark *tamāl* trees are splendorous with their bunches
of fresh sprouts and golden creepers that climb
and encircle them.

Temples bloom with trees of pinkish color, accented
here and there by flowering mango-saplings.

At the base of the trees are seen beautiful groups of rose-apple bushes, jackfruits and so many juicy limes.

The inner part of the forest is surrounded by groves
of banana trees.

Some are bearing ripe fruits while others bear
unripe green ones.

Rows and rows of coconut trees hold many, many fruits.

Among the rows of betel trees are date-palms and wood-apple trees.

There are sweet *jujube* berries, oranges, plums, plus
cardamom and clove vines.

All the fruit and flower-trees are so full with offerings
that their branches bend down and touch the
ground.
Pomegranates are bursting and soaking the ground
with their juice.
Hedges of jujube berries appear very beautiful.

There are so many varieties of trees that they
defy description!
In the center of the garden is a colorful temple.
Just in front of it is a lake full of cool waters.
The landing-steps are formed of crystal slabs.
On four sides are four bathing places inlaid with jewels.
Surrounding the lake are lilies-of-the-valley formed
of gold, white *sephalikā* flowers, golden *champaka*
creepers, and moonlike *mallikā* jasmines.
All these beautiful flowerbeds line the bank of the lake,
and their reflections can be seen in its pure waters.
From the weight of all the flowers, their stems bend
down and caress the surface of the water.
Sweet little ripples move along with the gentle breeze.
Lotuses of white, blue, red and much more
are in full bloom.
These lotuses sway so much that the bumblebees
cannot even land on them.
Greedy for honey, millions of bees fly all around.
Royal swans, storks, herons, partridges and
many other birds playfully sport in all directions.

The fish living within the water move about
by the hundreds.
In a golden temple, upon a golden altar sits Lord Gorā
of golden complexion.
Surrounding Him are His associates also of golden
complexion.
Their limbs tremble out of pure *prema*, and their eyes
are wet with tears.

There are twelve gates supported by reddish-
golden pillars.
On the outside are golden posts holding up
a nice canopy.
These gates are interwoven with garlands
of mallikā-jasmines.
The top edges have clusters of hanging sapphires
that sway to and fro.
The East courtyard has groves of divine Tulasī plants.
The West courtyard has groves of colorful flame-trees.
The North and South have grasses of dark *śyāmala* color
which bring to mind soft pillows to sit on.

Pet deer roam all about in search of grass to eat,
and they spread their eyes wide upon beholding
the beauty of Gaurāṅga.
A peacock alights from a magnolia tree upon seeing
Gorā there, and begins to dance in great happiness.
The trees and creepers all bloom with golden flowers.

The forest is perpetually served by the Six Seasons.
The sparrows chirp loudly, and the cuckoos are all-pervading.
Male and female waterfowl wander around on the ground.
Parrots see ripe *bimba* berries, and pick them with their beaks.
Bluebirds and doves sport within the trees.

Meditations on the Vrindāvan Pastimes

Female and male parrots call out: "Jai Śrī Śachī-Nandana!
Glory to the life and soul of Narahari and Gadādhara!
Glory, glory to the Lord of Lakshmī Vishnu-Priyā's life! Glory, glory to Rādhā and Krishna who have united in one form!
Glory, glory to He who has manifested all these desire-fulfilling trees!
Each and every one of our Vrindāvana-vāsīs has increased their *prema* unlimitedly by sporting here in Navadvīpa!"

Vishvambhara hears these statements of the parrots and remembers the *līlā* of Rādhā and Krishna at Rādhā-kunda within His mind:
One moment He says, "Who has stolen my flute?"
The next moment He says, "Just see! I have defeated you at dice!"

The next moment He says, "Let there be water-sports in this *kuṇḍa*!"

The next moment He says, "Come on! Let us go to the place of *Surya-pūjā!*"

The next moment He begins walking, holding Gadādhara's hand.

Thus He plays with His devotees in the flower garden.

They adorn Him with flower armlets, necklaces, and hair-ties.

They scatter flowers all around until the earth is completely covered.

The fragrance attracts thick swarms of bumblebees hovering about.

From moment-to-moment Prabhu goes to the base of each and every tree and sports there, being cooled by the shade.

They make relishable music as they play on *mridaṅgas* and *vīnās*.

Some dance and others make nice rhythms by clapping their hands.

The sweetness of this forest is equal to that of Vrindāvana, and the Lord eternally sports here with His associates.

Many groups of male servants clean up the groves.

It is impossible to describe these limitless forest-pastimes.

The servant of the servant of Śrī Gaurāṅga and Nityānanda, Krishna Dāsa, narrates the Lord's pastimes.

Thus Ends the Madhyāhna-Līlā

FIVE

Aparāhna-Līlā Afternoon Pastimes

(3:36 – 6:00 P.M.)

jaya jaya śrī chaitanya jaya nityānanda
jayādvaita-chandra jaya gaura-bhakta-vrinda

The Lord Tours the Town of Nadīyā

Then Gadādhara smiles and sweetly addresses the Lord,
"The afternoon time is approaching.
Śachī Mātā is very anxious for you.
She has labored to make many fine edibles.
Arranging them nicely on a golden plate, she waits and watches on the path for your return."

Hearing these words of Gadādhara, Prabhu says,
"Let us go!" and proceeds on His tour of the town.
As Gaurāṅga-Chanda approaches the outskirts,
both sides of Him are ornamented by
Nityānanda and Gadādhara.
Following behind is the assembly of devotees whose minds are all filled with bliss as they walk pleasantly.

As Gorā returns on the footpath to Nadīyā,
all the townspeople turn their heads
to behold His enchanting beauty.
His muscular, golden body is very tall, and its sheer
grace is like a lotus of pure desire in spotless waters.
His knee-length arms sway back and forth as he walks.
They appear as lotus-stems, or elephant trunks –
they cannot be described!
His curling tresses are so lovely they mesmerize
the entire universe, and they are tied with the
shyness of all the young girls.
His wavy locks swing like a swarm of bumblebees,
and the *chandan tilak* upon His forehead
diffuses rays just like a nectar-moon.
Fixing the flower-arrows of His restless eyes upon the
bow of His eyebrows, He instantly pierces the hearts
of the womenfolk by His mere glance.

The smile on his moonlike face showers the rains of
sweet ambrosia, which makes the *chakorī*-birds of
the womens' hearts greedily fly after it.
Jewelled *makarī*-shaped earrings swing from his ears,
making the *sapharī*-fish of the womens' hearts
pursue and swallow them.
The splendor of His neck and waist conquers
that of the lion.
These features of His vanquish the legend
of the chaste girls' *dharma*.
On His broad chest sway jewelled pearl necklaces
and matchless jasmine garlands.

His limbs are nicely smeared with thick patches
of Malayan sandalwood paste.
His clothing and ornaments enrapture the
entire universe!

Description of the Town

Prabhu now enters on the main road into Nadīyā,
and as the people hear of it, women, men,
young and old all run to see Him.
The sand on the road to Nadīyā is white as a
lotus flower, and on both sides rise lofty palaces
of pure white luster.
Banners with golden lotus symbols are touching the sky
as white, yellow and other colorful flags
blow in the wind.
The rooftop apartments are constructed with bewildering
optical illusions, and the gates to the houses
are festooned with swaying jasmine garlands.

All the women who live along the road that Gaurāṅga is
traversing ascend their rooftops with great desire
to behold Him.
Does it appear that a garland of nectar-moons is rising
in the sky with the clouds of their loosened hair
flowing by their cheeks?
Their jewelled necklaces appear like the rising stars, and
the waves of their smiles are the striking
of lightning.

Their soft chit-chatting is like the clouds' sweet gentle
rumbling, and their eyes are the lotuses
in the pond of affection.
The handsome body of Gaurāṅga is like a golden
mountain peak, upon which these girls shower
the rains of loving attachment.
From behind windows and portals some fix their eyes,
peering steadily down the path that Gaurāṅga
is traveling.

The town of Nadīyā extends for an area of four *yojanas*
(32 square miles). Here and there are flower gardens
and heavenly lakes.
All the palaces accommodate many temples of numerous
devatās, above which are splendorous rows and rows
of beautiful spires.

There are four classes of people – the *brāhmaṇas*,
kshatriyas, *vaishyas* and *shūdras*, and their lovely
homes shine in many orderly rows.
Uncountable *yogīs*, *sannyāsīs*, and *brahmachārīs*
live there.

In some places there is recitation of the *Bhagavad-gītā*
and the *Purāṇas*.
In some places is the excitement of dancing, singing,
and playing on musical instruments.
In some places small children loudly bicker
and squabble.
In some places uncountable older children are playing.

In some places numberless *vipras* study the scriptures.
In some places groups and groups of *bhattāchāryas* congregate to discuss philosophy.

Everyone walks along the roads of Nadīyā.
Three kinds of people travel on these roads – young, middle-aged and old – and they all gaze incessantly upon the face of Gaurāṅga.
Here and there are *kadamba* and *bakula* trees.
All around their bases are supremely splendorous sitting platforms.
The town has marketplaces, vestibules and courtyards packed with dense crowds of celestial people.
In the center of town are many, many mango trees, among which are perpetually blossoming flower gardens.
Surrounding the town are the flowing currents of the Sura-dhūni, upon whose banks Gaurāṅga sports enchanting pastimes.

The Glories of Navadvīpa

[From the *Chaitanya-Bhāgavat*]

"There is no town like Navadvīpa within the entire three worlds, for it is where Chaitanya Gosāi has taken birth.
Understanding that Prabhu was going to appear there, the Creator had made that place complete (sampūrṇa)."

O friends! Please listen to the meaning of the word '*sampūrṇa*.'

Everyone has not understood it, even after
contemplating it.
Great truth has been concentrated into very few letters.
If one ponders it, then priceless jewels will be gained.
Within the ocean are vast quantities of gemstones,
although the eyes can see nothing but water.
Sinful blind persons have no eyes to see anything
but water.
Even if they hear of something else,
they do not believe it.
Just as things within the ocean are not visible,
similarly the words of Vrindāvana Dāsa
have a deeper purpose.
No one can grasp the direct meaning of these statements
– but only one whose heart is attached to Gaura
can understand.
Some say that the word '*sampūrṇa*' indicates the
fourteen worlds.
Who can comprehend the sweetness of this
direct meaning?
It denotes the extent of all the pleasures in the universe
including beauty, majestic potency, and virtuous
conduct, plus the intoxicating essence of the topmost
limit of all knowledge, devotion, intelligence, wealth,
mercy, glorious family dynasties and so on, as well
as perfectly complete proficiency in the abilities of
relishing, and mastery of all forms of craftsmanship
– the word '*sampūrṇa*' is full of all these meanings.

Now there is yet another nectarean thing to speak of.
Hearing about it pleases one's ears and mind.

The following words have issued forth from the mouth of the son of Nārāyaṇī (Vrindāvana Dāsa Ṭhākura):

navadvīpa je heno mathurā rāja-dhānī

"This Navadvīpa is just like the opulent city of Mathurā."

Vrindāvan Dāsa is the object of Nityānanda Prabhu's mercy, who illumines him with the constant presence of His Divine Grace.
One who thinks he can understand Vrindāvana Dāsa's statements, is merely puffed-up with the illusory concept of scholarship, and simply dies while engrossed in the false ego.

[A song by Narahari Ghanashyāma]

(Refrain)

"Glories, glories to Śrī Nadīyā, the abode of happiness!
Peoples of the four ashrams dwell in wonderful homes
Where unparalleled festivals are observed according to custom.

It is the place where the eight mystic perfections and the nine opulences are the humble servant in every home.
Where those who are attached to dharma, artha, kāma and moksha are merely ridiculed.
Where the extremely severe threefold miseries are vanquished, and the ninefold processes of bhakti shine continuously.

Where the area is so full to overflowing with spotlessly pure prema that all the non-moving as well as the moving living beings remain everlastingly intoxicated in divine madness.
Where the town is beautified by thousands of diverse residences, and is encircled by the pure white waters of the Sura-dhūni.
Where young kunda-jasmine blossoms and strands of fine pearls appear as if a host of full moons have simultaneously arisen.
Where the overall splendor is new and ever-fresh just like Vrindāvana, and is served by six seasons that are succulent out to the horizon.
Where the charming and grand glories are so expansive that Shesha Nāga ever sings of them and never reaches their limit.
The best of the demigods, four-faced Lord Brahmā, in the company of the other devas, meditates on the exalted, limitless rasa manifest in this place.
Ghanashyāma narrates – may I eventually live in that place in the company of my Lord and His associates."

Mahāprabhu Sits on the Bank of the Gaṅgā

Thus Prabhu wanders about the town for awhile, then He proceeds on the path to the Sura-dhūni.
Coming to the bank of the Gaṅgā along with His associates, Mahāprabhu, the moon over Nadīyā, sits down near a bathing landing.

The bank of the Sura-dhūni shines with very beautiful
meadows where many *shāla*, *piyāla* and *kadamba*
trees grow.
There are peacocks, cuckoos and many bees flying
amongst flower-fields in thick swarms.
The bathing *ghāṭa* is paved step by step in stone slabs,
with countless Shiva shrines on the upper level.
Here and there are uncommon residential quarters,
in front of which flow the supremely pure waters.

Sitting on this Gaṅgā-*ghāṭa* is Gaurāṅga-Sundara.
His form of Madana-Mohana is captivating to all.
His charming face is continuously marked with smiles
as He jokes and converses with His own associates.
All the women who had come to get water from the river
give up their shyness and gaze continuously
upon the face of Gaurāṅga.
Some who were already carrying jugs full of water on
top of their heads – as soon as they behold Gorā
their hands slip from steadying their pots,
which fall and crash upon the ground.
Here and there are thousands and thousands of *vipras*
sitting in groups along with townswomen.
Also uncountable *bhattāchāryas* and their students
are congregating and discussing the scriptures
amongst themselves.
What grand splendor is manifest on both sides of this
Gaṅgā! Especially brilliant is the appearance
of Gorā-Chanda.

[**From the** *Chaitanya-Bhāgavat*]

"Sitting on the bank is Śrī Śachī-Nandana surrounded on four sides by His disciples.
It is just like Śrī Nanda-Kumāra on the bank of the Yamunā having fun amongst His cowherd boyfriends.
Krishna-Chandra has now taken His cowherd boyfriends, and sports numerous pranks in the form of a brāhmana on the bank of the Gaṅgā.
Those people who happen to look upon Prabhu's face there at the river obtain an absolutely indescribable type of happiness.
Affected by Prabhu's extremely potent and masterful influence, all the people on the bank of the Gaṅgā warmly embrace each other.
Glancing toward the teachers of the schools, Prabhu sits there and expounds His own commentaries.
Fortunate people watch as they surround Him on all sides, for by Prabhu's power, all of Navadvīpa is free from miseries."

Thus in the company of the devotees, Śrī Śachī-Nandana offers obeisance to the Gaṅgā and proceeds home.
Prabhu travels on the main road into Nadīyā during the time of the cows' return home.
Herds and herds of cows are entering the town, tended by hundreds and hundreds of cowherd boys.
Many calves playfully follow behind with their tails raised aloft.

Seeing this scene brings great delight to Prabhu's heart, and with a choked voice He calls out the names of Krishna's cows, *"O white Dhavalī!"* and so on.
Thousands upon thousands of *vipras* are coming on the path from the Gaṅgā to perform their *sandhyā* rituals at dusk.
Numberless young *brāhmaṇa* boys also proceed toward their homes making a tumultuous commotion as they recite and hear scriptural verses.

Prabhu returns to His own home and sits down as His devotees all go and return to their own homes also.
Then the bliss of Śachī Devī's heart swells up.
As she sees the face of her dear son, her ocean of happiness overflows.
Slowly and quietly she comes and sits before Gorā.
Overpowered with affection she wipes His limbs with her own cloth.

It is just like mother Yaśodā lovingly pampering Śrī Krishna.
Other than this comparison, there is none within the three worlds.

Thus Ends the Aparāhna-Līlā

SIX

Sāyaṁ-Līlā
Dusk Pastimes

(6:00 – 8:24 P.M.)

Gaurāṅga is Bathed and Then Worships the Deity

Then all the male-servants act very quickly, filling
golden pitchers with water and bringing them in.
One washes the Lord's feet. One combs out His hair
and ties it in a topknot.
His body is cleansed with scented water.
Finally rinsing Him again, they cover Him with fine
white cloth and offer Him fresh clothing
and ornaments.

Gaurahari then enters the temple of Lord Vishnu.
On Śachī's order, Devī Vishnu-Priyā lights a lamp
and goes into the temple.
On the altar is a *mūrti* of Raghunātha in the form of a
rock (*shīlā*).
Prabhu performs the *ārati* and bows down
to offer obeisances.
He brings and offers many gifts to the Deity.
Giving the image *āchaman* He then puts it to rest.

Gaurāṅga comes out of the temple and sits upon a divine
lion-throne as Śachī's bliss knows no bounds.
All the offerings that were presented to the Deity in the
Vishnu temple are saved separately for the evening.
Some items are brought out and placed before Śachī's son
and Prabhu smilingly eats in the greatest happiness.
After washing His mouth, Gaura Raya sits down
again as Vishnu-Priyā Devī remains nearby
to offer Him betel.

[From the *Chaitanya-Bhāgavat*]

*"Knowing the intense bliss of His mother's heart Prabhu
stays there and sits with Lakshmī"*

He Proceeds to Śrīvāsa's House

Then suddenly Prabhu becomes obsessed in his mind,
and He departs for Śrīvāsa's house.
What splendor is seen during this dusk time! In the four
directions is a great tumult of singing and music.
Brilliant lamps are lit by the streets in row after row,
making all the town spotlessly pure
by their effulgence.
Traveling on the path like a maddened lion,
Prabhu eventually arrives at Śrīvāsa's residence.
Seeing Prabhu come in, Śrīvāsa becomes very jubilant
and a great ecstasy blossoms among he and his
family members.

Bowing at His feet, they wash them, then take and seat Him upon a divine lion-throne.

The servant of the servant of Śrī Gaurāṅga and Nityānanda, Krishna Dāsa, narrates the Lord's pastimes.

Thus Ends the Sāyaṁ-Līlā

SEVEN

Pradosha-Līlā Evening Pastimes

(8:24 – 10:48 P.M.)

jaya jaya śrī chaitanya jaya nityānanda
jayādvaita-chandra jaya gaura-bhakta-vrinda

The Evening Ārati of Śrī Gaurāṅga

Then Nityānanda Prabhu arrives and meets
with everyone.
He sits to Mahāprabhu's right with his face blossoming.
Then comes Advaita-Chandra, the ocean of *prema*,
and Gadādhara, Narahari, Mukunda, Śrīdhara,
Vakreshvara, Haridāsa, and all the assembly
of devotees.
Everyone arrives quickly at Śrīvāsa's house.
Nityānanda Rāya holds an umbrella over the Lord's head.
On the left is Gadādhara waving a *chāmara* whisk.
Someone dances, someone sings, and someone
does *kīrtan*.
Someone lights a jewelled lamp and stands holding it.
Inside the house the womenfolk are chanting, "*Jaya!*

Jaya!" as the pleasant sounds of *mrīdangas*, *karatālas* and bells reverberate.
Advaita Gosāi lights a ghee lamp with five large wicks and performs *ārati* while his inner bliss knows no bounds.

[Thus a song by Narahari, to be sung in rāga Gaurī]

(Refrain)

"Glories, glories to the ārati of Gaura-Kishora.
Sporting upon a siṁhāsana, He appears to be a golden mountain.
Stealing the overflowing hearts of all the young women in the universe.
Śrī Advaita, brimming full of ecstatic prema, performs the ārati overwhelmed with delight while gazing upon his own Lord.
To the right is Nityānanda-Chandra, radiant with uncommon mannerisms, deeply absorbed in transcendental mellows.
To the left is Gadādhara striking elegant poses, holding up a new and brilliant umbrella.
Śrīvāsa throws showers and showers of flowers while Narahari continuously waves a chāmara whisk.
*Shuklāmbara daubs the Lord with chandan while Gupta Murāri shouts, '**Jaya!**'*
Mādhava, Vāsu Ghosha, Purushottama, Vijaya, Mukunda and other great souls of royal caliber are singing sweet rāgas endowed with matchless embellishments like shruti, mūrachana, grāma, sapta-svara and so forth.

They play expertly on mrīdaṅgas, tom-toms, small dampha drums, flutes, tiny high-pitched flutes, and more.
Bells and cymbals resound with loud ringing while deafening dish-shaped gongs clang out dense reverberations.
Vakreshvara dances in supreme exhilaration with luscious movements cavorting and spinning round and round.
Someone sings the rhythms **'thai thai thai'** *in various ways according to strictly precise musical rules.*
The rasikas Gadādhara, Śrīdhara, Gauridāsa and Haridāsa dance while overwhelmed and saturated with rasa.

"Gaura's face beams a sweet nectarean smile as He marvels, 'How wonderfully these devotees perform in extreme madness!'
The demigods in the sky are engrossed in this vision and their king Indra is able to leave only after great effort.
The husband of Parvatī and the four-faced one experience shivers of delight as copious tears continuously cascade from their eyes.
The three worlds are excitedly jubilant as Shesha chants descriptions of this scene, narrating the names of the participating munis and devotees.

"Narahari's Lord is the ornament of Vraja, saturated with rasa, the distributor of supremely matchless bliss in Nadīyā-pura."

All the Devotees Gather at Śrīvāsa's House

After completing the *ārati* ceremony, Advaita Ṭhākura shouts very loudly and begins dancing wildly.
All the other devotees that live in the area arrive one by one and meet with those already at Śrīvāsa's house.
Śachī Devī takes her daughter-in-law to the front of the house along with Sītā Devī and gathers with all the devotees' wives.
They stay in the house and gaze at the beauty of Gaurāṅga outside.
As Prabhu gestures, the devotees open the gate and allow His various associates entrance into the courtyard.

[From the *Chaitanya-Bhāgavat*]

"The door on the gate was opened only on the order of Prabhu so that no one other than His own associates could enter."

The son of Śachī sits smiling upon a *siṁhāsana*, attracting the minds of all by His own divine beauty and qualities.
Nityānanda, Gadādhara, Advaita, Śrīvāsa and everyone else continuously swims in the ocean of ecstatic love.
Upon the arrival of nightfall all become very jubilant and their moods are clearly revealed in their behavior.

Someone offers prayers, someone renders various services, someone offers palmfuls of flowers at the Lord's sacred feet.
Someone brings and presents diverse offerings.
Someone offers betel into His mouth while feeling limitless bliss.

Prabhu sits for a while enjoying the pleasure of Krishna-*kathā*.
This fathomless *Pradosha-Līlā* defies description!

The servant of the servant of Śrī Gaurāṅga and Nityānanda, Krishna Dāsa, narrates the Lord's pastimes.

Thus Ends the Pradosha-Līlā

EIGHT

Nishā-Līlā
Night Pastimes

(10:48 P.M. – 3:36 A.M.)

jaya jaya śrī-krishna-chaitanya nityānanda
jayādvaita-chandra jaya gaura-bhakta-vrinda

Lord Gaurāṅga Begins the Sankīrtan

Then Mahāprabhu's divine moonlike face beams in a wide smile and He gives the order to begin the *kīrtan.*

[From the *Chaitanya-Bhāgavat*]

"*Hearing this from the Lord, all the Vaishnavas were overjoyed, and thus Mahāprabhu began the grand sport of kīrtan.*
This kīrtan was held every night at Śrīvāsa's home, and occasionally at Chandra-Shekhara's.
Mukunda commenced with the auspicious invocation of the kīrtan and then chanted, **'Rama Krishna Narahari Gopāla Govinda!'**
Everyone was there – Nityānanda, Gadādhara, Advaita, Śrīvāsa, Vidyā-Nidhi, Murāri, Hiraṇya, Haridāsa, Gaṅgādāsa, Vanamālī, Vijaya-Nandana, Jagadānanda,

Buddhimanta Khān, Nārāyaṇa, Kāshīshvara,
Vāsudeva, Rāma, Garuḍa, Govinda, Govindānanda,
Gopīnātha, Jagadīsha, Śrīman, Śrīdhara, Sadāshiva,
Vakreshvara, Bhūgarbha, Shuklāmbara, Brahmānanda,
Purushottama, Sañjaya, and so on –
uncountable servants of Śrī Chaitanya were there –
I know them all by name.
All of them were present together during Prabhu's dancing,
and other than His own personal associates,
no one else was there.
Hearing the loud shouting of Prabhu, mixed with the cries
of **'Hari! Hari!'** *in the night – it was as if the universe*
was being split open.
All the sinful souls were perishing in this tumult
as Śachī-Nandana ecstatically performed His kīrtan.
Seeing everyone forcefully tumbling and falling upon the
ground, Govinda Dāsa came forward and shut his eyes.
Sometimes Prabhu manifested Himself in the mood of God,
and sometimes He would weep and exclaim, 'I am but a
lowly servant!'
Thus in the sacred courtyard of Śrīvāsa, the auspicious
uproar of kīrtan arose with the names
'Gopāla! Govinda!'*"*

The Ecstatic Chanting and Dancing Escalates

"Śrīvāsa took charge of one group as Mukunda took another
and ran this way and that.
Govinda Datta took charge of yet another, and everyone did
kīrtan as Gaura-Chandra danced.

Sometimes the greatly muscular Nityānanda would grab
hold of Him as Advaita secretly took the dust of His feet.
Gadādhara and his group had tearful eyes and were
completely overcome with bliss by Prabhu's kīrtan.

When Prabhu Vishvambhara danced and stomped
vigorously on the ground, the earth trembled
and everyone scattered in fear.
Sometimes as Vishvambhara danced at a moderate pace,
He appeared to be Nanda-Nandana, the best of dancers.
The next moment, meditating inwardly He would hold His
hands as if He were playing a flute, and thus looked
exactly like Vrindāvana-Chandra Himself.
When He manifested this mood it was totally astonishing,
as the son of Jagannātha Mishra was suspended
in the bliss of His own names.
From moment-to-moment great perspiration would flow
from His pores, appearing like the Gaṅgā had
personally come out from His body.
Seeing Prabhu's ecstatic bliss, the Bhāgavata devotees
held each others' necks and wept.

The divine limbs of everyone were smeared with divine
chandan, and they were adorned with flower garlands.
Ecstatically chanting Krishna's name, they forgot all else
in the world.
The sounds of the mridaṅgas, small finger-cymbals,
and conchshells mixed with the saṅkīrtana
in a thunderous blend of excitement.
This tumult arose in the universe and filled the sky,
vanquishing inauspiciousness in all directions.

What a wonder that upon the dancing of Whose servants, all troubles were destroyed and the universe was made pure!
This Prabhu personally danced to the chanting of His own holy names.
What is the result of all this? These pastimes of Śrī Gaurāṅga were foretold in the ancient Purāṇas.

In four directions resounded the most auspicious Śrī Harināma-Sankīrtana, and in the middle danced the son of Jagannātha Mishra.

Absorbed in the bliss of Whose holy name, Lord Shiva does not know that he is naked –
By Whose name Lord Brahma dances, while He Himself also dances –
By Whose name Valmikī became a great ascetic –
By Whose name Ajāmila was liberated –
Whose name is taken by Shuka and Nārada as they wander –
Whose glories are sung by Shesha of a thousand mouths – in the bliss of His own names dances Prabhu Vishvambhara.

The rhythm of His feet striking the earth is most enchanting. Prabhu looks at all the Vaishnavas one by one.
Overcome with ecstatic moods, the devotees loudly repeat the names of the Lord's previous incarnations.

Even Lord Haladhara, Shiva, Shuka, Nārada, Prahlāda, Lakshmī, Aja, and Uddhava all chanted along with this kīrtan.

As before, great care is taken that no outsiders enter
the courtyard and behold this scene.
Just as so many yugas elapsed during the performance of
the Mahā-rāsa dance – all the gopīs in this present
incarnation now consider such a length of time to pass
like half a mustard-seed.

In this way Krishna's inconceivable manifestation
blossomed, and only the fortunate servants
of Śrī Chaitanya could come here."

[There is a poem in this regard]

"Jaya re! Jaya re!
Gorā Śrī Śachī-Nandana of lovely form dances auspiciously!
His qualities are sung in ecstatic kīrtan by Śrīvāsa,
Rāmānanda, Mukunda and Vāsu.
The drums resound, **'dram drimiki drimiki drimi'** *as the*
relishable finger-cymbals chime along sweetly.
The hearts of His associates are pierced by flower-arrows,
overwhelming them in ecstatic moods."

The Glories of Gadādhara Paṇḍita

[A song by Lochana Dāsa Thakura]

"Glories, glories to Gadādhara and Gaurāṅga-Sundara!
They are one soul manifest in two separate bodies! Rādhā
and Krishna, the fresh young couple of Vrndāvan, have
now appeared here as Gadādhara and Gaura-Chandra.

Rādhā Vrindāvaneshvarī is the personification
of mahā-bhāva – She has now incarnated
as Gadādhara Paṇḍita
And Vrajendra-Nandana is the personification of the King
of Rasa – He has fully manifested as this
Gaura-Chandra.

One who endeavors to worship on the rāgānuga-mārga,
the path of spontaneous devotion, follows the disciples
of Paṇḍita Gosāi (Gadādhara Paṇḍita).
Without following them, Vraja cannot be attained.
Therefore the Goswamis of Vraja are branches
of this disciplic succession.
He whom Lakshmī Devī meditates upon, even executing
austerities for the purpose of attaining Him, but still not
attaining her desire – this Vrajendra-Nandana
is truly loved by Rādhā.
Indeed, She is overwhelmed with prema for Him
at every moment, and now this Rādhā has become
Paṇḍita Gosāi, who is madly engrossed in the
nectar-mellows of Gaura-prema.
Therefore one who is devoid of attachment to Gadādhara
cannot attain prema-bhakti, but instead becomes
totally destitute.
If someone does not believe in this principle, he cannot be
delivered for a million births, and is completely ruined.

My prayer at the feet of Gadādhara-Gaurāṅga is that I have
never had association with Your true followers;
I have been pleased to associate with sinful atheists, and

I am pierced by the spears of Gadādhara Paṇḍita's blasphemers;
My mind is full of attachment to drinking liquor, and I have frightfully kept the company of other drunkards;
Still, perpetually hoping for the lotus feet of Gadādhara-Gaura, Lochana Dāsa begs for shelter under these feet."

❦ ❦ ❦

[Another song by Lochana Dāsa]

"Dear mind, just worship, just worship the son of Madhava known as Gadādhara!
Whoever takes shelter of his lotus feet goes to Vraja-dhāma.
Previously he appeared in Vrishabhānu's house at Vraja-pura bearing the name Rādhikā.
In the company of Her girlfriends, fond of playful pranks, She serves Shyama and makes Him happy.
That form is now this form, the same Queen of relishable mellows.
Just worship Her incessantly with single-minded attention!
Now in the company of Gaura, She has incarnated and sports playfully in the dress of a renounced male ascetic.
Coming to Nilāchala and living in the company of many devotees, Gadādhara has delivered many countries.
The entire universe is swimming in the flood of prema that he has brought, which vanquished all the miseries of everyone.

But this sinful soul has never seen that ocean of prema, says Lochana Dāsa."

[Another song by Lochana Dāsa]

"In hope for Gadādhara, Gadādhara, Gadādhara – if you attain Gadādhara you get residence in Vraja-pura.
Taking the name of Gadādhara, I will become an ascetic.
I will eat from my water pot and wear a simple loincloth.
These are the hopes of my mind for many days now.
With my ears I will hear about Gadādhara-Gaura-prema.
Dear Lords! Those who know You can be a guru or a disciple in Your lineage.
Only persons bereft of eyes reject You and uselessly attempt to perform devotional service.
One who is devoid of attachment to Gadādhara's lotus feet remains fallen in the ocean of birth and death.

In hope of attaining the lotus feet of Gadādhara, Lochana Dāsa begs for remembrance of those feet."

[Another poem]

"Re! Some say that Gorā is Jānakī-vallabha (Lord Rāma), or the beloved of Rādhā (Lord Krishna), or Pañcha Vaṇa (Cupid with five flower arrows).
But in the mind of the poet Nayanānanda, I know nothing other than this – that Gaura is the life and soul of my Gadādhara. Re!"

The Kīrtan is Concluded

Thus Gaurāṅga-Sundara frolics in the happiness of
kīrtan as the late night enters the second *prahara*.
After some time Prabhu stops the chanting
and sits in the courtyard with His devotees.
His dear companions wave fans to alleviate
the fatigue of the *kīrtan*.
Śachī Devī takes Lakshmī Vishnu-Priyā along
and quickly leaves for home.
The other family members of the *bhaktas* also happily
leave for their own residences.

Arriving at home, Śachī Devī bids her daughter-in-law
goodnight and goes inside, feeling boundless bliss.
Then Śachī begins to prepare edibles and fixes her eyes
on the path where Gorā will appear.
Gaurāṅga bids farewell to all the devotees and proceeds
toward His own home.

On some nights after *kīrtan* during the Summertime,
He bathes in the Gaṅgā with the devotees
in the moonlight.

Arriving at home, servants wipe His body with fine
damp cloths to relieve His fatigue from sporting so
much chanting and dancing during the *kīrtan*.

Changing Him into fresh clothes, they wash His sacred
feet, and He sits upon an *āsana* to take *prasād*.
Śachī Devī brings numerous offerings on golden trays
and places them within the sight of her son.
She comes over and sits before Him to behold His face,
and overflowing with pure loving affection,
she eagerly urges Him to feast again and again.
Prabhu eats while smiling gently as Lakshmi Vishnu-
Priyā looks on, filling her eyes.

Finishing His meal, Prabhu washes His mouth, and
sitting in a solitary place He chews betel nuts.
Then He goes to His sleeping-chamber and lies down
to rest upon the opulent bed.
Whatever food remnants are leftover from Prabhu's plate
are honored by Lakshmi Vishnu-Priyā.
All the servants headed by Īshana clean the house
and go to take rest in their own quarters.
Then Lakshmī Vishnu-Priyā quickly goes to the Lord's
chamber and secretly serves His lotus feet.

[**From the** ***Chaitanya-Bhāgavat***]

*"After eating, Prabhu chews betel and goes to lie down
while Lakshmī takes His feet."*

On some days, the devotees headed by Haridāsa and
Gadādhara also rest in Prabhu's house.
Nityānanda Prabhu comes here and takes his meal,
resting afterwards in great delight.
Advaita, Śrī Gadādhara, Vakreshvara, Śrīvāsa,

Śrī Narahari and all the other associates go
to take rest in their own homes.
Having their meals, they finally go to sleep.

[**From the** ***Chaitanya-Bhāgavat***]

"These pastimes are being performed by Gaura Rāya even up to the present moment. Occasionally some fortunate souls catch a glimpse of it."

In the dead of night, all becomes still as Gaurāṅga-Sundara happily falls asleep.

The servant of the servant of Śrī Gaurāṅga and Nityānanda, Krishna Dāsa, narrates the Lord's pastimes.

Thus Ends the Nishā-Līlā

Thus Ends Śrī Gaurāṅga-Līlāmṛta

Publisher's Note

The idea to reissue *Śrī Gaurāṇga-Līlāmṛta*, translated by Daśaratha-Suta Dāsa in 1992, came when we lent our Nectar Books' edition to a young friend. After reading it, she wanted a copy of her own, only to find out that this book and most others published by Nectar Books were out of print – with no chance they would be back in print in any foreseeable future.

We found this to be an unfortunate turn of events and so we approached Daśaratha-Suta to suggest that Bookwrights Press could republish some of his Nectar Books' title list, with updated editing, designs, and bindings. Hopefully, this could bring these rare, but important manuscripts to a new audience. He was eager to see the books back in circulation and gracious enough to allow us to take the reins.

Unfortunately, he had no computer files for this title. Amit Ācāra Dāsa kindly took on the task of rekeying the whole text from our hard copy; Gāndharvikā Keli Devī Dasī expertly proofread the work; and yours truly supplied the cover and text design.

Please watch for other Bookwrights Press republications of Daśaratha-Suta Dāsa's translations, as well as books by other Vaishnava authors.

Māyāpriyā Devī Dasī
Publisher

Made in United States
North Haven, CT
03 March 2022

16657542R00059